English Master

C1 Key Word Transformation

Margaret Cooze

20 practice tests for the
Cambridge C1 Advanced

PROSPERITY EDUCATION

PROSPERITY EDUCATION

www.prosperityeducation.net

Registered offices: Sherlock Close, Cambridge
CB3 0HP, United Kingdom

© Prosperity Education Ltd. 2020

First published 2020

ISBN: 978-1-916-129-757

Manufactured on demand by KDP.

For further information and resources, visit:
www.prosperityeducation.net

Ad infinitum et ultra

Contents

Introduction

Welcome to this edition of sample tests for the Cambridge C1 Advanced, Part 4: Key Word Transformation, designed specifically for students preparing for the challenging Use of English section of the (CAE) examination, but also suitable for any English language student working at CEFR C1 level.

The pass threshold of the Cambridge C1 Advanced (CAE) examination is 60% and so, in order to allow ample time for the reading parts (Parts 5–8) of Paper 1, it is advisable that candidates complete The Use of English section (Parts 1–4) as quickly as possible while maintaining accuracy.

This resource contains 200 exam-styled, single-sentence assessments, each carrying a lexical/lexico-grammatical focus, testing lexis, grammar and vocabulary. Each assessment comprises a sentence, followed by a 'key' word and an alternative sentence conveying the same meaning as the first but with a gap in the middle. Use the key word provided to complete the second sentence so that it has a similar meaning to the first sentence. You cannot change the keyword provided. Each correct answer is broken down into two marks. Next to each sentence transformation answer you will find a guide indicating the focus of the two parts of the answer: either G (grammatical) or L (lexical). This is a rough indication to help you with your revision for the exam.

Author **Margaret Cooze** taught extensively in the UK and abroad before moving into academic management and teacher training. She holds an MA in Applied Linguistics and an MSc in English Language Teaching Management, and has worked in senior roles at Cambridge English Language Assessment and Cambridge Assessment International Education.

The content in this volume is also available in the English Master C1 mobile app, part of a suite of critically acclaimed, test-practice learning tools geared towards the Cambridge B2 First and C1 Advanced Use of English and Listening exams.

Visit www.prosperityeducation.net to see our wide range of print and digital resources, and free exam-practice materials.

Michael Macdonald
Prosperity Education, Cambridge

PROSPERITY EDUCATION
www.prosperityeducation.net

Cambridge C1 Advanced
Use of English

Part 4

Test 1

For questions 1–10, complete the second sentence, using the word given, so that it has a similar meaning to the first sentence. Do not change the word provided and use between three and six words in total. In the separate answer sheet, write your answers in capital letters, using one box per letter.

1   Every single suggestion I made was felt to be impossible.

    DEEMED

    All of _____ be possible.

2   I expect we will be found in the end.

    DARE

    I _____ us eventually.

3   I do not think I have ever seen such a bad film.

    RANK

    That _____ film I have ever seen.

4   The team members were annoyed as they were not consulted.

    LACK

    It was _____ members of the team.

5 We would have had to get up at 6am, if we had walked all the way.

MEANT

Walking from start _____ up at 6am.

6 In your position I would have accepted the invitation.

SHOES

If I had _____ not have declined the invitation.

7 I regret coming to such an awful restaurant.

FOOT

I wish I _____ restaurant as awful as this.

8 It is scary to think of the possible outcome.

THINK

I _____ have happened.

9 After some time he agreed to the police interviewing him.

CONSENT

He gave _____ by the police eventually.

10 He was proud of his skillful work.

PRIDE

He _____ so skillfully.

Answer sheet: Key word transformation   Test No. [   ]

Name _____   **Date** _____

Write your answers in capital letters, using one box per letter.

1

2

3

4

5

6

7

8

9

10

Mark out of 20 [   ]

Cambridge C1 Advanced Use of English

Part 4

Test 2

For questions 1–10, complete the second sentence, using the word given, so that it has a similar meaning to the first sentence. Do not change the word provided and use between three and six words in total. In the separate answer sheet, write your answers in capital letters, using one box per letter.

1   How would you manage if you could not drive?

    INCAPABLE

    Suppose you _____, what would you do?

2   He clearly believes he has the whole committee on his side.

    UNDER

    He _____ on the committee supports him.

3   If she applies and gets turned down, I am sure it will be disappointing for her.

    DISAPPOINTED

    She is sure _____ is unsuccessful.

4   My assumption will be that you will let me know if you are coming.

    ASSUME

    If I do not hear _____ you are not coming.

5 The situation was serious, but he seemed not to understand that.

GRAVITY

I really do not _____ the situation.

6 My mother is very good at buying the perfect gifts for people.

FAILS

My mother _____ are perfect for people.

7 I've noticed that his swimming has got much better recently.

MARKED

There has been _____ recently.

8 I always thought the place she lived would be like this.

IMAGINED

This is exactly what _____ be like.

9 Although it is expensive, all the evidence suggests that it will sell well.

EVERY

Despite the expense _____ that people will buy it.

10 I only found out about our burglary on Tuesday.

BEEN

I didn't _____ until Tuesday.

Answer sheet: Key word transformation   Test No. [ ]

Name _____   **Date** _____

Write your answers in capital letters, using one box per letter.

1

2

3

4

5

6

7

8

9

10

Mark out of 20 [ ]

Cambridge C1 Advanced Use of English

Part 4

Test 3

For questions 1–10, complete the second sentence, using the word given, so that it has a similar meaning to the first sentence. Do not change the word provided and use between three and six words in total. In the separate answer sheet, write your answers in capital letters, using one box per letter.

1 It was the most cowardly decision they could have made.

LACK

They showed _____ decision-making.

2 He has always had everything he ever desired.

WANTED

He has _____ his life.

3 Giving people news that is bad is never easy.

BREAK

It's always _____ someone.

4 I was impressed by the standard of the acting.

OF

The acting _____ standard.

5 People say that the facts are hidden.

COVER

There is said _____ of the facts.

6 My lasting memory is of how hard he tried to help his family.

LENGTHS

I always _____ to for his family.

7 Despite being reduced, the car is not cheap enough.

REMAINS

Even though it is reduced, the _____ too expensive.

8 As soon as the play started, I knew it would be boring.

OUTSET

I was sure from _____ bored by the play.

9 That way of cooking became unpopular many years ago.

FELL

Cooking like _____ a long time ago.

10 The phone rang and then immediately afterwards she arrived at the door.

HAD

No _____ than she arrived at the door.

Answer sheet: Key word transformation

Test No. ☐

Name _____   **Date** _____

Write your answers in capital letters, using one box per letter.

1

2

3

4

5

6

7

8

9

10

Mark out of 20 ☐

Cambridge C1 Advanced
Use of English

Part 4

Test 4

For questions 1–10, complete the second sentence, using the word given, so that it has a similar meaning to the first sentence. Do not change the word provided and use between three and six words in total. In the separate answer sheet, write your answers in capital letters, using one box per letter.

1   Following these directions will ensure you will not get lost.

    FOLLOW

    As _____ these directions, you will not get lost.

2   If I miss this meeting, nobody will let me forget it.

    LIVE

    I _____ if I miss this meeting.

3   My decision was not go shopping with him.

    AGAINST

    I _____ with him.

4   It wasn't possible for him to move all the parcels in the time he had on his own.

    PROVED

    Working _____ all the parcels within the timeframe.

5 There is a risk that she will not finish her essay on time.

DANGER

She is _____ her essay in time.

6 I thought it was unfair of her to resent me for forgetting her birthday.

HOLD

I do not think she _____ I forgot her birthday.

7 I wonder if we would benefit from a new name for our shop.

DO

Maybe our _____ a new name.

8 This month a few more people have attended meetings.

SLIGHTLY

There has _____ at meetings this month.

9 How likely is it that he will get the job, do you think?

CHANCES

What do you think the _____ the job are?

10 It has snowed much more heavily here this year than it has for ten years.

HAVE

Over the past year we _____ in the previous decade.

Answer sheet: Key word transformation

Test No. [ ]

Name _____ **Date** _____

Write your answers in capital letters, using one box per letter.

1

2

3

4

5

6

7

8

9

10

Mark out of 20 [ ]

Cambridge C1 Advanced Use of English

Part 4

Test 5

For questions 1–10, complete the second sentence, using the word given, so that it has a similar meaning to the first sentence. Do not change the word provided and use between three and six words in total. In the separate answer sheet, write your answers in capital letters, using one box per letter.

1   I was more impressed by the acting than I expected to be.

   EXCEEDED

   The thing _____ the acting.

2   Yesterday the weather was too hot for me to go jogging.

   HEAT

   If it _____ I would have gone jogging yesterday.

3   For far too long she hasn't been appreciated.

   GRANTED

   She _____ for ages.

4   It's important that I ask the builder to fix the door.

   FIXED

   I must _____ the builder.

5 He complained that I had been too loud in the meeting.

ACCUSED

I _____ too loud in the meeting.

6 However much he studied he couldn't remember the poem.

MATTER

He had trouble _____ how hard he studied.

7 I blame the weather for the fact that people did not come to the play.

DOWN

The lack of attendance _____ the weather.

8 This book is so awful that I'm about to give up on it.

VERGE

I am _____ up on this awful book.

9 I think it may rain tomorrow.

RAINED

I wouldn't _____ tomorrow.

10 Do not lend your identify card to anyone.

CIRCUMSTANCES

Under _____ borrow your identity card.

Answer sheet: Key word transformation   Test No. ☐

Name _____   **Date** _____

Write your answers in capital letters, using one box per letter.

1 ☐☐☐☐☐☐☐☐☐☐☐☐☐☐☐
   ☐☐☐☐☐☐☐☐☐☐☐☐☐☐☐

2 ☐☐☐☐☐☐☐☐☐☐☐☐☐☐☐
   ☐☐☐☐☐☐☐☐☐☐☐☐☐☐☐

3 ☐☐☐☐☐☐☐☐☐☐☐☐☐☐☐
   ☐☐☐☐☐☐☐☐☐☐☐☐☐☐☐

4 ☐☐☐☐☐☐☐☐☐☐☐☐☐☐☐
   ☐☐☐☐☐☐☐☐☐☐☐☐☐☐☐

5 ☐☐☐☐☐☐☐☐☐☐☐☐☐☐☐
   ☐☐☐☐☐☐☐☐☐☐☐☐☐☐☐

6 ☐☐☐☐☐☐☐☐☐☐☐☐☐☐☐
   ☐☐☐☐☐☐☐☐☐☐☐☐☐☐☐

7 ☐☐☐☐☐☐☐☐☐☐☐☐☐☐☐
   ☐☐☐☐☐☐☐☐☐☐☐☐☐☐☐

8 ☐☐☐☐☐☐☐☐☐☐☐☐☐☐☐
   ☐☐☐☐☐☐☐☐☐☐☐☐☐☐☐

9 ☐☐☐☐☐☐☐☐☐☐☐☐☐☐☐
   ☐☐☐☐☐☐☐☐☐☐☐☐☐☐☐

10 ☐☐☐☐☐☐☐☐☐☐☐☐☐☐☐
    ☐☐☐☐☐☐☐☐☐☐☐☐☐☐☐

Mark out of 20   ☐

Cambridge C1 Advanced
Use of English

Part 4

Test 6

For questions 1–10, complete the second sentence, using the word given, so that it has a similar meaning to the first sentence. Do not change the word provided and use between three and six words in total. In the separate answer sheet, write your answers in capital letters, using one box per letter.

1   You must consider everyone's opinion before you make a decision.

ACCOUNT

All options _____ before a decision is made.

2   After the talk tomorrow the author will be answering questions.

OPPORTUNITY

Tomorrow's author talk will _____ to ask her questions.

3   She was really delighted to find the lost book last week.

MUCH

Last week, _____ the book she had lost.

4   The public have been asked to check their bank notes for forgeries by the police.

LOOKOUT

Police have asked the public _____ the forged banknotes.

5   The concerns of the residents have led to some detailed planning.

   DRAWN

   Detailed plans _____ address the concerns of
   the residents.

6   The team winning the football match by such a big score was a complete
   surprise to everyone.

   EMPHATICALLY

   The fact that the team _____ was surprising to all.

7   She approached the farm with anxiety.

   WAY

   Anxiously, _____ towards the farm.

8   The offer he made scared me too much for me to accept it.

   TAKE

   I was too scared _____ his offer.

9   It was a shame that she did not like the restaurant.

   LIKING

   The restaurant _____ I am afraid to say.

10   Danny was the best player and was given a prize this week as well as last week.

   AWARDED

   Danny _____ being the best player for the last two weeks.

Answer sheet: Key word transformation

Test No. [ ]

Name _____ **Date** _____

Write your answers in capital letters, using one box per letter.

1 [ ][ ][ ][ ][ ][ ][ ][ ][ ][ ][ ][ ][ ][ ][ ]
[ ][ ][ ][ ][ ][ ][ ][ ][ ][ ][ ][ ][ ][ ][ ]

2 [ ][ ][ ][ ][ ][ ][ ][ ][ ][ ][ ][ ][ ][ ][ ]
[ ][ ][ ][ ][ ][ ][ ][ ][ ][ ][ ][ ][ ][ ][ ]

3 [ ][ ][ ][ ][ ][ ][ ][ ][ ][ ][ ][ ][ ][ ][ ]
[ ][ ][ ][ ][ ][ ][ ][ ][ ][ ][ ][ ][ ][ ][ ]

4 [ ][ ][ ][ ][ ][ ][ ][ ][ ][ ][ ][ ][ ][ ][ ]
[ ][ ][ ][ ][ ][ ][ ][ ][ ][ ][ ][ ][ ][ ][ ]

5 [ ][ ][ ][ ][ ][ ][ ][ ][ ][ ][ ][ ][ ][ ][ ]
[ ][ ][ ][ ][ ][ ][ ][ ][ ][ ][ ][ ][ ][ ][ ]

6 [ ][ ][ ][ ][ ][ ][ ][ ][ ][ ][ ][ ][ ][ ][ ]
[ ][ ][ ][ ][ ][ ][ ][ ][ ][ ][ ][ ][ ][ ][ ]

7 [ ][ ][ ][ ][ ][ ][ ][ ][ ][ ][ ][ ][ ][ ][ ]
[ ][ ][ ][ ][ ][ ][ ][ ][ ][ ][ ][ ][ ][ ][ ]

8 [ ][ ][ ][ ][ ][ ][ ][ ][ ][ ][ ][ ][ ][ ][ ]
[ ][ ][ ][ ][ ][ ][ ][ ][ ][ ][ ][ ][ ][ ][ ]

9 [ ][ ][ ][ ][ ][ ][ ][ ][ ][ ][ ][ ][ ][ ][ ]
[ ][ ][ ][ ][ ][ ][ ][ ][ ][ ][ ][ ][ ][ ][ ]

10 [ ][ ][ ][ ][ ][ ][ ][ ][ ][ ][ ][ ][ ][ ][ ]
[ ][ ][ ][ ][ ][ ][ ][ ][ ][ ][ ][ ][ ][ ][ ]

Mark out of 20 [ ]

25

Cambridge C1 Advanced
Use of English

Part 4

Test 7

For questions 1–10, complete the second sentence, using the word given, so that it has a similar meaning to the first sentence. Do not change the word provided and use between three and six words in total. In the separate answer sheet, write your answers in capital letters, using one box per letter.

1   Once he had made his mind up, she knew she could not change it.

     POSSIBILITY

     She was sure _____ his mind.

2   Did you not want me to show people the new car?

     RATHER

     Would _____ people the new car?

3   He really could not give an explanation for the missing money.

     LOSS

     He _____ the missing money.

4   It is probable that they will rush to make some decisions at the meeting.

     RESULT

     The meeting is _____ rushed decisions.

5 The woman acted quickly and managed to stop the fight.

PART

Quick action _____ the woman stopped the fight.

6 Would you be able to look after my dog today?

WONDERING

I _____ would mind looking after my dog today.

7 I do not think it will happen, but if you do not like the dress, you can return it.

EVENT

You can return the dress _____ you do not like it.

8 Despite having an accident, my sister will not stop driving.

INTENTION

My sister _____ up driving after her accident.

9 "It was hard to think of new ideas for my new book", said the author.

COME

The author admitted that it _____ with new ideas for his new book.

10 That team is almost sure to win the match this weekend.

EVERY

The team stands _____ the match this weekend.

Answer sheet: Key word transformation

Test No. [ ]

Name _____   **Date** _____

Write your answers in capital letters, using one box per letter.

1 □□□□□□□□□□□□□□□
   □□□□□□□□□□□□□□□

2 □□□□□□□□□□□□□□□
   □□□□□□□□□□□□□□□

3 □□□□□□□□□□□□□□□
   □□□□□□□□□□□□□□□

4 □□□□□□□□□□□□□□□
   □□□□□□□□□□□□□□□

5 □□□□□□□□□□□□□□□
   □□□□□□□□□□□□□□□

6 □□□□□□□□□□□□□□□
   □□□□□□□□□□□□□□□

7 □□□□□□□□□□□□□□□
   □□□□□□□□□□□□□□□

8 □□□□□□□□□□□□□□□
   □□□□□□□□□□□□□□□

9 □□□□□□□□□□□□□□□
   □□□□□□□□□□□□□□□

10 □□□□□□□□□□□□□□□
   □□□□□□□□□□□□□□□

Mark out of 20 [ ]

Cambridge C1 Advanced
Use of English

Part 4

Test 8

For questions 1–10, complete the second sentence, using the word given, so that it has a similar meaning to the first sentence. Do not change the word provided and use between three and six words in total. In the separate answer sheet, write your answers in capital letters, using one box per letter.

1   We need at least five more people to get a football team together.

    FEWER

    To complete the football team, _____ people are needed.

2   It has taken me more than an hour to finish all the ironing.

    SPENT

    I _____ all of the ironing.

3   She was surprised to be awarded the prize for writing the best essay.

    CAME

    The prize for the _____ to her.

4   I think Jane has been on a diet as she looks so slim now.

    MUST

    Jane looks so slim that _____ on a diet.

5 She started crying when she was told about the accident.

BROKE

Upon hearing _____ in tears.

6 Do you mind if I borrow your bicycle?

OBJECTION

Do you _____ borrowing your bicycle?

7 I have never thought about buying a new car.

OCCURRED

It _____ that I should buy a new car.

8 I hope Sarah makes a decision about whether to accept the job soon.

MIND

I think Sarah ought _____ about the job offer soon.

9 One day I am sure I will win a game!

MATTER

It is only _____ beat him at tennis!

10 I think learning to play the piano is a waste of time.

POINT

In my opinion _____ to play the piano.

Answer sheet: Key word transformation   Test No. ☐

Name _____   **Date** _____

Write your answers in capital letters, using one box per letter.

1

2

3

4

5

6

7

8

9

10

Mark out of 20 ☐

Cambridge C1 Advanced Use of English

Part 4

Test 9

For questions 1–10, complete the second sentence, using the word given, so that it has a similar meaning to the first sentence. Do not change the word provided and use between three and six words in total. In the separate answer sheet, write your answers in capital letters, using one box per letter.

1   They started to dig the ditch as soon as they arrived.

     LOST

     When they arrived they _____ to dig the ditch.

2   This is the most complicated set of instructions in my opinion.

     CONCERNED

     As _____ this set of instructions is the most

     complicated.

3   It makes me irritated when people talk on their phones in the cinema.

     NERVES

     It gets _____ talking on their phones in the

     cinema.

4   I cannot remember anything about being in the accident.

     RECOLLECTION

     I have _____ in the accident.

5 The warning sign was ignored by nearly every child.

TOOK

Hardly any _____ of the warning sign.

6 There are not many tickets so you cannot guarantee you will get one.

COUNT

You should _____ of the tickets as there are not many.

7 I might be able to afford those shoes.

PRICE

It is possible that those _____ range.

8 He was really pleased to win the award.

DELIGHT

Much to _____ the award.

9 When she acted in that big movie she became famous.

NAME

She _____ after acting in that big movie.

10 As a child I always hated vegetables.

HATE

I _____ I was a child.

Answer sheet: Key word transformation

Test No. [ ]

Name _____ **Date** _____

Write your answers in capital letters, using one box per letter.

1 [ ][ ][ ][ ][ ][ ][ ][ ][ ][ ][ ][ ][ ][ ][ ]
[ ][ ][ ][ ][ ][ ][ ][ ][ ][ ][ ][ ][ ][ ][ ]

2 [ ][ ][ ][ ][ ][ ][ ][ ][ ][ ][ ][ ][ ][ ][ ]
[ ][ ][ ][ ][ ][ ][ ][ ][ ][ ][ ][ ][ ][ ][ ]

3 [ ][ ][ ][ ][ ][ ][ ][ ][ ][ ][ ][ ][ ][ ][ ]
[ ][ ][ ][ ][ ][ ][ ][ ][ ][ ][ ][ ][ ][ ][ ]

4 [ ][ ][ ][ ][ ][ ][ ][ ][ ][ ][ ][ ][ ][ ][ ]
[ ][ ][ ][ ][ ][ ][ ][ ][ ][ ][ ][ ][ ][ ][ ]

5 [ ][ ][ ][ ][ ][ ][ ][ ][ ][ ][ ][ ][ ][ ][ ]
[ ][ ][ ][ ][ ][ ][ ][ ][ ][ ][ ][ ][ ][ ][ ]

6 [ ][ ][ ][ ][ ][ ][ ][ ][ ][ ][ ][ ][ ][ ][ ]
[ ][ ][ ][ ][ ][ ][ ][ ][ ][ ][ ][ ][ ][ ][ ]

7 [ ][ ][ ][ ][ ][ ][ ][ ][ ][ ][ ][ ][ ][ ][ ]
[ ][ ][ ][ ][ ][ ][ ][ ][ ][ ][ ][ ][ ][ ][ ]

8 [ ][ ][ ][ ][ ][ ][ ][ ][ ][ ][ ][ ][ ][ ][ ]
[ ][ ][ ][ ][ ][ ][ ][ ][ ][ ][ ][ ][ ][ ][ ]

9 [ ][ ][ ][ ][ ][ ][ ][ ][ ][ ][ ][ ][ ][ ][ ]
[ ][ ][ ][ ][ ][ ][ ][ ][ ][ ][ ][ ][ ][ ][ ]

10 [ ][ ][ ][ ][ ][ ][ ][ ][ ][ ][ ][ ][ ][ ][ ]
[ ][ ][ ][ ][ ][ ][ ][ ][ ][ ][ ][ ][ ][ ][ ]

Mark out of 20 [ ]

Cambridge C1 Advanced
Use of English

Part 4

Test 10

For questions 1–10, complete the second sentence, using the word given, so that it has a similar meaning to the first sentence. Do not change the word provided and use between three and six words in total. In the separate answer sheet, write your answers in capital letters, using one box per letter.

1   Being the strongest swimmer has always been the most important thing for her.

   OBSESSED

   She _____ being the strongest swimmer.

2   James told me that, finally, work was getting better.

   LOOKING

   James said _____ at work at last.

3   She hid the fact that she was ill from him.

   DARK

   She managed _____ about her illness.

4   I do not think I have much chance of getting the job.

   HOPE

   I have given _____ given the job.

5 Her piano playing is getting better and better.

GOOD

She is _____ learning the piano.

6 The bus went without him as he did not rush to get it.

SENSE

He had _____ and missed the bus.

7 Sales have gone up massively over the past 12 months.

DRAMATIC

There _____ in sales this year.

8 I do not feel like going cycling today.

MOOD

I am not _____ my bike today.

9 Just now he is not worried about anything at all.

WORLD

He does not _____ at the moment.

10 Although she was criticised, she made the decision to carry on working.

PRESS

She decided _____ despite the criticism.

Answer sheet: Key word transformation

Test No. ☐

Name _____ **Date** _____

Write your answers in capital letters, using one box per letter.

1 ☐☐☐☐☐☐☐☐☐☐☐☐☐☐☐
  ☐☐☐☐☐☐☐☐☐☐☐☐☐☐☐

2 ☐☐☐☐☐☐☐☐☐☐☐☐☐☐☐
  ☐☐☐☐☐☐☐☐☐☐☐☐☐☐☐

3 ☐☐☐☐☐☐☐☐☐☐☐☐☐☐☐
  ☐☐☐☐☐☐☐☐☐☐☐☐☐☐☐

4 ☐☐☐☐☐☐☐☐☐☐☐☐☐☐☐
  ☐☐☐☐☐☐☐☐☐☐☐☐☐☐☐

5 ☐☐☐☐☐☐☐☐☐☐☐☐☐☐☐
  ☐☐☐☐☐☐☐☐☐☐☐☐☐☐☐

6 ☐☐☐☐☐☐☐☐☐☐☐☐☐☐☐
  ☐☐☐☐☐☐☐☐☐☐☐☐☐☐☐

7 ☐☐☐☐☐☐☐☐☐☐☐☐☐☐☐
  ☐☐☐☐☐☐☐☐☐☐☐☐☐☐☐

8 ☐☐☐☐☐☐☐☐☐☐☐☐☐☐☐
  ☐☐☐☐☐☐☐☐☐☐☐☐☐☐☐

9 ☐☐☐☐☐☐☐☐☐☐☐☐☐☐☐
  ☐☐☐☐☐☐☐☐☐☐☐☐☐☐☐

10 ☐☐☐☐☐☐☐☐☐☐☐☐☐☐☐
   ☐☐☐☐☐☐☐☐☐☐☐☐☐☐☐

Mark out of 20 ☐

Cambridge C1 Advanced Use of English

Part 4

Test 11

For questions 1–10, complete the second sentence, using the word given, so that it has a similar meaning to the first sentence. Do not change the word provided and use between three and six words in total. In the separate answer sheet, write your answers in capital letters, using one box per letter.

1   I was urged to make my decision based on the facts alone.

BASE

My sister encouraged me not _____ anything that was not factual.

2   I chose not to attend the last lecture of the day as it was not relevant to me.

OPTED

Due to _____ out of the last lecture of the day.

3   It will not help if we queue up now.

BLIND

Joining the queue now _____ of difference.

4   I was surprised when I saw her coming out of the shop.

EXITING

Seeing _____ a surprise.

5 She discovered that everyone else knew about the plan.

DARK

She found out that she was the _____ about the plan.

6 I have not been to this town since my childhood.

HAVE

Not since I _____ to this town.

7 I got the impression that John would accompany me to the meeting.

BELIEVE

I was _____ attending the meeting with John.

8 The fact that the restaurant had new owners was news to me.

TAKEN

I was not aware that the restaurant _____ new owners.

9 I am sure that my book is better than yours.

MIND

There is _____ that your book is not as good as mine.

10 She stood there until she could no longer see the car any more.

OUT

She did not move _____ her sight.

Answer sheet: Key word transformation   Test No. [   ]

Name _____   **Date** _____

Write your answers in capital letters, using one box per letter.

1

2

3

4

5

6

7

8

9

10

Mark out of 20   [   ]

Cambridge C1 Advanced Use of English

Part 4

Test 12

For questions 1–10, complete the second sentence, using the word given, so that it has a similar meaning to the first sentence. Do not change the word provided and use between three and six words in total. In the separate answer sheet, write your answers in capital letters, using one box per letter.

1   Having a good reputation in this area of business is important when choosing a company.

REGARDED

It is important to choose a company _____ in this area of business.

2   Not as many people live in big houses these days.

COMMON

It is not _____ be for people to live in big houses.

3   I was so surprised when I saw what was in the box.

OF

Seeing the _____ as a complete surprise.

4   I persuaded her it was too much to spend on the present.

OUT

I _____ so much on the present.

5 Seeing people running from the building shocked me.

SHOCK

Much _____ people running from the building.

6 You must ask me if you want any help with things.

HESITATE

Please _____ for help if you need anything.

7 He said he would not tolerate any noise from the students.

PUT

"I will not _____ noisy," he said.

8 No changes are being made to the plans for the project.

AHEAD

The project _____ plan.

9 You should hurry up because the train is about to leave.

POINT

The train is _____ so you should hurry up.

10 It is extremely unlikely that we will win the match.

CHANCE

There is almost _____ winning the match.

Answer sheet: Key word transformation

Test No. [ ]

Name _____ **Date** _____

Write your answers in capital letters, using one box per letter.

1

2

3

4

5

6

7

8

9

10

Mark out of 20 [ ]

Cambridge C1 Advanced Use of English

Part 4

Test 13

For questions 1–10, complete the second sentence, using the word given, so that it has a similar meaning to the first sentence. Do not change the word provided and use between three and six words in total. In the separate answer sheet, write your answers in capital letters, using one box per letter.

1   I really wanted to participate in the play at our school.

   PART

   I always longed _____ school play.

2   He trusted that the process was fair.

   FAITH

   He put _____ process.

3   Eating the right balance of food is very important in staying healthy.

   DIET

   A _____ importance in maintaining good health.

4   He was motivated to learn the language when he moved to the country.

   WITH

   Moving to another country provided _____ to learn the language.

5 I wrote a note and put it on the door to remind him about the meeting.

JOG

So as _____ I put a note about the meeting on the door.

6 To his disappointment, the parade was cancelled.

BITTERLY

He was _____ of the parade.

7 Avoiding doing the washing up was her aim.

OUT

She aimed _____ the washing up.

8 He demanded an apology from the rude woman.

APOLOGISE

He insisted _____ being so rude.

9 She was late but still managed to catch the train.

CATCHING

She _____ in spite of being later.

10 I worry that she is finding that medication addictive.

BECOMING

I am afraid _____ that medication.

Answer sheet: Key word transformation   Test No. ☐

Name _____   **Date** _____

Write your answers in capital letters, using one box per letter.

1

2

3

4

5

6

7

8

9

10

Mark out of 20 ☐

Cambridge C1 Advanced
Use of English

Part 4

Test 14

For questions 1–10, complete the second sentence, using the word given, so that it has a similar meaning to the first sentence. Do not change the word provided and use between three and six words in total. In the separate answer sheet, write your answers in capital letters, using one box per letter.

1   I am expecting a lot from today's course.

   EXPECTATIONS

   I have _____ course today.

2   My plan is to make my room brighter by adding some new lighting.

   UP

   I plan _____ some new lighting.

3   I am so grateful for all your help.

   ENOUGH

   I cannot _____ me so much.

4   I plan to get up later tomorrow as I am really tired.

   HAVING

   I am so tired that I plan _____ tomorrow.

5 He took the decision to accept the offer they made.

TAKE

He decided _____ their offer.

6 There is nothing I hate more than a messy kitchen.

MORE

I hate an _____ else.

7 That was the biggest challenge ever for Peter.

FACED

Peter _____ a big challenge.

8 They decided to abolish school uniform in her school.

DO

The decision _____ away with school uniform in her school.

9 Defending herself against all those aggressive people was brave.

STAND

It was brave _____ to so many aggressive people.

10 The owners of this shop should think about staying open longer.

BENEFIT

The shop owners would _____ opening hours.

Answer sheet: Key word transformation   Test No. ☐

Name _____   **Date** _____

Write your answers in capital letters, using one box per letter.

1

2

3

4

5

6

7

8

9

10

Mark out of 20 ☐

Cambridge C1 Advanced
Use of English

Part 4

Test 15

For questions 1–10, complete the second sentence, using the word given, so that it has a similar meaning to the first sentence. Do not change the word provided and use between three and six words in total. In the separate answer sheet, write your answers in capital letters, using one box per letter.

1   If they employed more people it would be a good idea.

ACTION

The best plan _____ employ more people.

2   People worldwide recognise how important recycling is.

CAUGHT

The importance of _____ over the world.

3   He did not have enough money to join them on holiday.

AFFORD

He _____ holiday with them.

4   Although my flight was cancelled, I was able to get on the next one.

SUBSEQUENT

I managed to get _____ mine was cancelled.

5 I am absolutely sure of her innocence.

MIND

There is _____ that she is innocent.

6 He was the most dependable member of the team.

DEPEND

You _____ than anyone else in the team.

7 That area has a lot of houses very close together.

DENSELY

It is _____ area.

8 Meeting everyone was the most important thing for her.

LENGTHS

She _____ sure to meet everyone.

9 I do not think he deserves all this attention.

GETTING

The attention he _____ in my opinion.

10 Someone might run the race faster than anyone else has done at the next Olympic Games.

COULD

The world record _____ at the next Olympic Games.

Answer sheet: Key word transformation

Test No. [ ]

Name _____ **Date** _____

Write your answers in capital letters, using one box per letter.

1

2

3

4

5

6

7

8

9

10

Mark out of 20 [ ]

Cambridge C1 Advanced Use of English

Part 4

Test 16

For questions 1–10, complete the second sentence, using the word given, so that it has a similar meaning to the first sentence. Do not change the word provided and use between three and six words in total. In the separate answer sheet, write your answers in capital letters, using one box per letter.

1   She said that she would not help him anymore.

    DONE

    She said that _____ helping him.

2   I am not sure I can find a solution to the problem.

    CONFIDENCE

    I do not _____ the problem.

3   People think that this house is the oldest one in town.

    THOUGHT

    It _____ oldest house in the town.

4   I would really like a good cup of coffee.

    ANYTHING

    What _____ is a good cup of coffee.

5 She became a vet because she was so caring.

SUCH

If she _____ person she would not have become a vet.

6 Do contact us if you need to know anything else.

FURTHER

Should _____ let us know.

7 An invoice will be sent to you after the job is complete.

UPON

They will send _____ the job.

8 I feel that the police will catch the hijackers.

BOUND

The police _____ who hijacked the plane.

9 Many people believe that this policy will fail.

BE

It is widely _____ unsuccessful.

10 Someone broke this car's window recently.

BROKEN

The window of _____ times.

Answer sheet: Key word transformation

Test No. [   ]

Name _____ **Date** _____

Write your answers in capital letters, using one box per letter.

1

2

3

4

5

6

7

8

9

10

Mark out of 20 [   ]

Cambridge C1 Advanced
Use of English

Part 4

Test 17

For questions 1–10, complete the second sentence, using the word given, so that it has a similar meaning to the first sentence. Do not change the word provided and use between three and six words in total. In the separate answer sheet, write your answers in capital letters, using one box per letter.

1   To maintain a record of the shop's visitors, the owners set up a video camera.

    TRACK

    The owners of the shop _____ the shop by installing a video camera.

2   He said he would contact me again, but he never did.

    TOUCH

    Despite promising _____ I never heard from him again.

3   I had no hesitation in recommending them.

    TWICE

    I did not _____ recommendation.

4   That was not really what I meant.

    MIND

    That was not quite _____ to be honest.

5 The police refused to let us cross the road because of the accident.

PREVENTED

Due to the accident, _____ the road by the police.

6 I must improve my skills in Excel before I start that course.

BRUSH

I need _____ Excel skills for that course.

7 I have been told that it is a very historical city.

STEEPED

The city _____ from what I've heard.

8 He has a lot of self-confidence in his ability to lead a team.

LACK

He does not suffer _____ his team-leading skills.

9 Apparently more people at that hotel have become sick.

REPORTED

More people _____ ill at that hotel.

10 Due to the fact that he didn't have relevant experience, I decided not to accept his offer of help.

GROUNDS

I rejected his offer to help _____ he did not have the necessary experience.

Answer sheet: Key word transformation   Test No. [   ]

Name _____   **Date** _____

Write your answers in capital letters, using one box per letter.

1 [ ][ ][ ][ ][ ][ ][ ][ ][ ][ ][ ][ ][ ][ ]
    [ ][ ][ ][ ][ ][ ][ ][ ][ ][ ][ ][ ][ ][ ]

2 [ ][ ][ ][ ][ ][ ][ ][ ][ ][ ][ ][ ][ ][ ]
    [ ][ ][ ][ ][ ][ ][ ][ ][ ][ ][ ][ ][ ][ ]

3 [ ][ ][ ][ ][ ][ ][ ][ ][ ][ ][ ][ ][ ][ ]
    [ ][ ][ ][ ][ ][ ][ ][ ][ ][ ][ ][ ][ ][ ]

4 [ ][ ][ ][ ][ ][ ][ ][ ][ ][ ][ ][ ][ ][ ]
    [ ][ ][ ][ ][ ][ ][ ][ ][ ][ ][ ][ ][ ][ ]

5 [ ][ ][ ][ ][ ][ ][ ][ ][ ][ ][ ][ ][ ][ ]
    [ ][ ][ ][ ][ ][ ][ ][ ][ ][ ][ ][ ][ ][ ]

6 [ ][ ][ ][ ][ ][ ][ ][ ][ ][ ][ ][ ][ ][ ]
    [ ][ ][ ][ ][ ][ ][ ][ ][ ][ ][ ][ ][ ][ ]

7 [ ][ ][ ][ ][ ][ ][ ][ ][ ][ ][ ][ ][ ][ ]
    [ ][ ][ ][ ][ ][ ][ ][ ][ ][ ][ ][ ][ ][ ]

8 [ ][ ][ ][ ][ ][ ][ ][ ][ ][ ][ ][ ][ ][ ]
    [ ][ ][ ][ ][ ][ ][ ][ ][ ][ ][ ][ ][ ][ ]

9 [ ][ ][ ][ ][ ][ ][ ][ ][ ][ ][ ][ ][ ][ ]
    [ ][ ][ ][ ][ ][ ][ ][ ][ ][ ][ ][ ][ ][ ]

10 [ ][ ][ ][ ][ ][ ][ ][ ][ ][ ][ ][ ][ ][ ]
     [ ][ ][ ][ ][ ][ ][ ][ ][ ][ ][ ][ ][ ][ ]

Mark out of 20 [   ]

Cambridge C1 Advanced Use of English

Part 4

Test 18

For questions 1–10, complete the second sentence, using the word given, so that it has a similar meaning to the first sentence. Do not change the word provided and use between three and six words in total. In the separate answer sheet, write your answers in capital letters, using one box per letter.

1   A party to celebrate Jane's birthday is being organised by her friends.

THROWING

Jane's friends _____ party to celebrate her birthday.

2   He always taps his fingers on the desk when he is on the phone, which is annoying.

STOP

I wish _____ the desk with his fingers when he's on the phone.

3   You can only learn to play the piano well with daily practice.

EVERY

Only _____ can you become a really good pianist.

4   I like to make sure I am fully informed about any new place I visit.

UP

I think it's important to _____ I haven't visited before.

5 Thankfully the car stopped or there could have been an awful event.

COULD

I dread _____ if the car had not stopped.

6 All the students helped out in tidying the school after the accident.

PITCHED

Every _____ the school after the accident.

7 He took the decision to leave when he realised what had happened.

ON

When it eventually _____, he decided to leave.

8 This year they have made a lot of people redundant.

LAID

A large number of people _____ this year.

9 Every now and again there is snow in my town.

INTERMITTENTLY

It _____ where I live.

10 It is usual for this company to pay an annual bonus to employees.

RULE

In this company, _____ bonus at the end of the year.

Answer sheet: Key word transformation

Test No. [   ]

Name _____ **Date** _____

Write your answers in capital letters, using one box per letter.

1 [ ][ ][ ][ ][ ][ ][ ][ ][ ][ ][ ][ ][ ][ ][ ]
      [ ][ ][ ][ ][ ][ ][ ][ ][ ][ ][ ][ ][ ][ ][ ]

2 [ ][ ][ ][ ][ ][ ][ ][ ][ ][ ][ ][ ][ ][ ][ ]
      [ ][ ][ ][ ][ ][ ][ ][ ][ ][ ][ ][ ][ ][ ][ ]

3 [ ][ ][ ][ ][ ][ ][ ][ ][ ][ ][ ][ ][ ][ ][ ]
      [ ][ ][ ][ ][ ][ ][ ][ ][ ][ ][ ][ ][ ][ ][ ]

4 [ ][ ][ ][ ][ ][ ][ ][ ][ ][ ][ ][ ][ ][ ][ ]
      [ ][ ][ ][ ][ ][ ][ ][ ][ ][ ][ ][ ][ ][ ][ ]

5 [ ][ ][ ][ ][ ][ ][ ][ ][ ][ ][ ][ ][ ][ ][ ]
      [ ][ ][ ][ ][ ][ ][ ][ ][ ][ ][ ][ ][ ][ ][ ]

6 [ ][ ][ ][ ][ ][ ][ ][ ][ ][ ][ ][ ][ ][ ][ ]
      [ ][ ][ ][ ][ ][ ][ ][ ][ ][ ][ ][ ][ ][ ][ ]

7 [ ][ ][ ][ ][ ][ ][ ][ ][ ][ ][ ][ ][ ][ ][ ]
      [ ][ ][ ][ ][ ][ ][ ][ ][ ][ ][ ][ ][ ][ ][ ]

8 [ ][ ][ ][ ][ ][ ][ ][ ][ ][ ][ ][ ][ ][ ][ ]
      [ ][ ][ ][ ][ ][ ][ ][ ][ ][ ][ ][ ][ ][ ][ ]

9 [ ][ ][ ][ ][ ][ ][ ][ ][ ][ ][ ][ ][ ][ ][ ]
      [ ][ ][ ][ ][ ][ ][ ][ ][ ][ ][ ][ ][ ][ ][ ]

10 [ ][ ][ ][ ][ ][ ][ ][ ][ ][ ][ ][ ][ ][ ][ ]
      [ ][ ][ ][ ][ ][ ][ ][ ][ ][ ][ ][ ][ ][ ][ ]

Mark out of 20 [   ]

Cambridge C1 Advanced
Use of English

Part 4

Test 19

For questions 1–10, complete the second sentence, using the word given, so that it has a similar meaning to the first sentence. Do not change the word provided and use between three and six words in total. In the separate answer sheet, write your answers in capital letters, using one box per letter.

1   It is not often that she is on time for class.

   TENDENCY

   She _____ up late for class.

2   Annoyingly, he can be seen chatting outside the office every day.

   BASIS

   I see him chatting outside the office _____ annoying.

3   Helping them is not something you have to do.

   OBLIGATION

   You are not _____ them.

4   He tends to tell people what to do.

   LAW

   He is always _____ about things.

5 He does exactly what he wants and ignores all the rules.

APPLY

He always thinks that _____ to him.

6 It's pointless to be so inflexible.

DIGGING

There is _____ heels in.

7 Using this machinery like that was dangerous.

INJURY

You could _____ on this machinery.

8 This might be the only chance you ever get to travel worldwide.

ONCE

This could be _____ chance to travel around the world.

9 Would you mind if I asked you a question?

PICK

Could I _____ something?

10 Paul thinks that Mary is not capable of doing the job.

UP

Paul does _____ the job.

Answer sheet: Key word transformation

Test No. ☐

Name _____ **Date** _____

Write your answers in capital letters, using one box per letter.

1 ⬚⬚⬚⬚⬚⬚⬚⬚⬚⬚⬚⬚⬚⬚⬚
⬚⬚⬚⬚⬚⬚⬚⬚⬚⬚⬚⬚⬚⬚⬚

2 ⬚⬚⬚⬚⬚⬚⬚⬚⬚⬚⬚⬚⬚⬚⬚
⬚⬚⬚⬚⬚⬚⬚⬚⬚⬚⬚⬚⬚⬚⬚

3 ⬚⬚⬚⬚⬚⬚⬚⬚⬚⬚⬚⬚⬚⬚⬚
⬚⬚⬚⬚⬚⬚⬚⬚⬚⬚⬚⬚⬚⬚⬚

4 ⬚⬚⬚⬚⬚⬚⬚⬚⬚⬚⬚⬚⬚⬚⬚
⬚⬚⬚⬚⬚⬚⬚⬚⬚⬚⬚⬚⬚⬚⬚

5 ⬚⬚⬚⬚⬚⬚⬚⬚⬚⬚⬚⬚⬚⬚⬚
⬚⬚⬚⬚⬚⬚⬚⬚⬚⬚⬚⬚⬚⬚⬚

6 ⬚⬚⬚⬚⬚⬚⬚⬚⬚⬚⬚⬚⬚⬚⬚
⬚⬚⬚⬚⬚⬚⬚⬚⬚⬚⬚⬚⬚⬚⬚

7 ⬚⬚⬚⬚⬚⬚⬚⬚⬚⬚⬚⬚⬚⬚⬚
⬚⬚⬚⬚⬚⬚⬚⬚⬚⬚⬚⬚⬚⬚⬚

8 ⬚⬚⬚⬚⬚⬚⬚⬚⬚⬚⬚⬚⬚⬚⬚
⬚⬚⬚⬚⬚⬚⬚⬚⬚⬚⬚⬚⬚⬚⬚

9 ⬚⬚⬚⬚⬚⬚⬚⬚⬚⬚⬚⬚⬚⬚⬚
⬚⬚⬚⬚⬚⬚⬚⬚⬚⬚⬚⬚⬚⬚⬚

10 ⬚⬚⬚⬚⬚⬚⬚⬚⬚⬚⬚⬚⬚⬚⬚
⬚⬚⬚⬚⬚⬚⬚⬚⬚⬚⬚⬚⬚⬚⬚

Mark out of 20 ☐

Cambridge C1 Advanced
Use of English

Part 4

Test 20

For questions 1–10, complete the second sentence, using the word given, so that it has a similar meaning to the first sentence. Do not change the word provided and use between three and six words in total. In the separate answer sheet, write your answers in capital letters, using one box per letter.

1   He is always very negative about everything.

    LOOK

    He can never _____ side of things.

2   He was surprised at her foolish actions.

    BELIEVE

    He could _____ foolish.

3   In winter, there is a tendency for the field by the river to flood.

    PRONE

    That field by the river _____ in winter.

4   The speaker told us that there were two aims of the meeting.

    TWOFOLD

    "The purpose _____," said the speaker.

5 The car costs more than I think it should, considering it is so old.

OLD

When you think _____ car is overpriced.

6 I think it is a good idea to go to the dentist once a year.

DENTIST

In my opinion _____ is sensible.

7 Hardly anyone writes letters since the internet started.

ADVENT

Since _____, people rarely write letters.

8 I do not mind telling you that I'm a fan of soap operas!

ASHAMED

I like soap operas and I am _____ it!

9 It is hard to survive without a mobile phone these days.

HAVE

Anyone _____ a mobile phone nowadays will struggle in daily life.

10 He is feeling sick because he ate too quickly.

UNWELL

He would not _____ eaten more slowly.

Answer sheet: Key word transformation   Test No. ☐

Name _____   **Date** _____

Write your answers in capital letters, using one box per letter.

1 ☐☐☐☐☐☐☐☐☐☐☐☐☐☐☐
☐☐☐☐☐☐☐☐☐☐☐☐☐☐☐

2 ☐☐☐☐☐☐☐☐☐☐☐☐☐☐☐
☐☐☐☐☐☐☐☐☐☐☐☐☐☐☐

3 ☐☐☐☐☐☐☐☐☐☐☐☐☐☐☐
☐☐☐☐☐☐☐☐☐☐☐☐☐☐☐

4 ☐☐☐☐☐☐☐☐☐☐☐☐☐☐☐
☐☐☐☐☐☐☐☐☐☐☐☐☐☐☐

5 ☐☐☐☐☐☐☐☐☐☐☐☐☐☐☐
☐☐☐☐☐☐☐☐☐☐☐☐☐☐☐

6 ☐☐☐☐☐☐☐☐☐☐☐☐☐☐☐
☐☐☐☐☐☐☐☐☐☐☐☐☐☐☐

7 ☐☐☐☐☐☐☐☐☐☐☐☐☐☐☐
☐☐☐☐☐☐☐☐☐☐☐☐☐☐☐

8 ☐☐☐☐☐☐☐☐☐☐☐☐☐☐☐
☐☐☐☐☐☐☐☐☐☐☐☐☐☐☐

9 ☐☐☐☐☐☐☐☐☐☐☐☐☐☐☐
☐☐☐☐☐☐☐☐☐☐☐☐☐☐☐

10 ☐☐☐☐☐☐☐☐☐☐☐☐☐☐☐
☐☐☐☐☐☐☐☐☐☐☐☐☐☐☐

Mark out of 20 ☐

Answers

1	my suggestions were		deemed not to	L	G
2	dare say	they will find / someone will find / that they will find / that someone will find		L	G
3	must rank as / has to rank as		the worst	L	G
4	the lack of consultation		that annoyed / which annoyed	L	G
5	to finish		would have meant getting	L	G
6	been in your shoes		I would	L	G
7	had never / had not		set foot in a	G	L
8	hate to think / dread to think		what could / might / may	L	G
9	his consent		to being interviewed / an interview	L	G
10	took pride / had pride		in doing his work / in working	L	G

1	were incapable		of driving	G	G
2	is under the impression		that everyone / everyone	L	L
3	to be disappointed		if her application	G	L
4	from you		I will assume / I will assume that	L	G
5	think he understood		the gravity of	G	L
6	never fails to choose		gifts that	G	G
7	a marked improvement		in his swimming	L	G
8	I imagined	her house would / her home would		G	G
9	there is	every indication / every chance / every possibility		G	L
10	find out		we had been burgled	L	G

1	a lack of bravery	in their		L	G
2	never wanted for (always had)	anything in (everything he wanted in)		L	G
3	hard to break / difficult to break	bad news to		G	L
4	was of	an impressive		G	L
5	to be	a cover up		G	L
6	remember the (great) lengths / recall the (great) lengths	he went		L	L
7	fact remains	that the car is		L	G
8	the outset	that I would be		L	G
9	that	fell out of favour / fell out of fashion		G	L
10	sooner had	the phone rung		G	G

1	long as	you follow		G	G
2	will never	live it down		G	L
3	decided against	going shopping		L	G
4	alone it proved / alone proved	impossible to move		L	L
5	in danger of	not finishing		L	G
6	should hold it against	me that / me because		L	G
7	shop could	do with		G	L
8	been a slightly	higher attendance		G	L
9	chances of	him getting		L	G
10	have had / have seen	more snowfall than / more snow than		G	L

1	that exceeded	my expectations was	G	L
2	had not been	for the heat	G	L
3	has been	taken for granted	G	L
4	get the door	fixed by	G	L
5	was accused	of being	G	G
6	remembering the poem	no matter	G	L
7	at the play	was down to	G	L
8	on the verge	of giving	L	G
9	be surprised	if it rained	L	G
10	no circumstances	should you let anyone / let anyone	L	G

1	must be taken	into account	G	L
2	be followed	by an opportunity	G	L
3	much to her delight	she found	L	G
4	to be	on the lookout	G	L
5	are being / have been	drawn up to	G	L
6	won the football match / won the match	so emphatically	G	L
7	she made	her way	G	L
8	to take him	up on	L	L
9	was not to	her liking	G	L
10	has been awarded	the prize for	G	L

1	there was no possibility	of changing	L	G
2	you rather	I had not shown	G	G
3	was at a loss	to explain	L	G
4	likely to	result in / result in some	L	L
5	on the	part of	L	L
6	was wondering	if you / whether you	G	G
7	in the	unlikely event that	L	L
8	has no intention	of giving	L	G
9	had been hard	to come up	G	L
10	every chance	of winning	L	G

1	no fewer than	five more	L	L
2	have spent	over an hour doing	G	L
3	best essay	came as a surprise	L	L
4	she must	have been	G	G
5	about the accident	she broke down	G	L
6	have any	objection to me / objection to my	G	L
7	has never occurred	to me	G	G
8	to make	up her mind / her mind up	G	L
9	a matter of time	until I / before I	L	L
10	there is no point / there is little point	in learning	L	G

1	lost no time	in starting	L	G
2	far as	I am concerned	L	G
3	on my nerves	to hear people	L	G
4	no recollection	of being	L	G
5	of the children / children	took any notice	L	G
6	not count on	getting one	L	G
7	shoes are within	my price	L	L
8	his delight	he won	L	G
9	made a name	for herself	L	G
10	used to hate	vegetables when	G	L

1	has always been	obsessed with	G	L
2	that things were	looking up / looking better	G	L
3	to keep him	in the dark	L	L
4	up hope	of being	L	G
5	making good	progress with / progress in	G	L
6	no sense	of urgency	L	L
7	has been a	dramatic increase / dramatic rise	G	L
8	in the mood	to ride	L	G
9	have a care	in the world	G	L
10	to press on / press ahead	with her work / with the work	L	L

1	to base	my decision on	G	L
2	a lack of relevance / its irrelevance	I opted	L	L
3	will not make	a blind bit	G	L
4	her exiting	the shop was / the shop came as	G	G
5	only person / only one	in the dark	L	L
6	was a child	have I been	G	G
7	led to believe	I would be	L	G
8	had been	taken over by	G	L
9	no doubt	in my mind	L	L
10	until the car	was out of	L	G

1	that is		highly regarded / well regarded	G	L
2	as common as		it used to	G	G
3	contents of the		box came	L	L
4	talked her out		of spending	L	G
5	to my shock		I saw	L	G
6	do not hesitate		to ask	L	G
7	put up with	any student being / any students being		L	G
8	is going ahead		according to	G	L
9	on the point		of leaving	L	G
10	no chance		of us	L	G

1	to take part	in our / in the	L	G
2	his faith	in the	L	G
3	balanced diet / well balanced diet	is of vital / is of great	L	G
4	him with	the motivation	G	L
5	to jog	his memory	G	L
6	bitterly disappointed	about the cancellation / by the cancellation	L	L
7	to get out	of doing	L	G
8	that the woman / the woman	apologise for	G	L
9	succeeded in	catching the train	L	G
10	she is becoming	addicted to	G	L

1	high expectations	of the	L	L
2	to brighten up	my room with	G	L
3	thank you enough	for helping	L	G
4	on having	a lie in / a long lie	G	L
5	to take them	up on	G	L
6	untidy kitchen	more than anything	L	G
7	had never	faced such	G	L
8	was made / was taken	to do	G	L
9	of her	to stand up	G	L
10	benefit from	lengthening their / lengthening the / longer	L	L

1	of action		would be to	L	G
2	recycling has		caught on all	G	L
3	could not afford		to go on	G	G
4	(on) the subsequent / onto the subsequent	flight after / flight when		L	G
5	no doubt		in my mind	L	L
6	could depend		on him more	G	L
7	a very		densely populated	G	L
8	went to great lengths		to be	L	G
9	is getting		is underserved	G	L
10	for the race		could be broken	L	G

1	she was		done with	G	L
2	have confidence that / have confidence		I can solve / in solving	L	L
3	is thought		that this is the / this is the	G	G
4	I would like / I want		more than anything	G	L
5	had not been		such a caring	G	L
6	you need / you require	any further information / any further details / to know anything further		G	L
7	you an invoice		upon completion of	G	L
8	are bound to	catch the men/people/women/individuals		L	G
9	believed that this / believed this		policy will be	G	G
10	this car was / the car was		broken in recent	G	G

1	kept track of	the visitors to / visitors to / people visiting	L	L
2	to keep / to stay	in touch	L	L
3	think twice about	giving them a	L	G
4	what I had	in mind	G	L
5	we were prevented	from crossing	G	G
6	to brush up	on my / my	L	L
7	is steeped	in history	G	L
8	from a	lack of confidence in	L	L
9	are reported / have been reported	to have fallen / to have become	G	G
10	on the	grounds that	L	L

1	are throwing	her a	G	G
2	he would	stop tapping	G	G
3	by practising	every day	G	L
4	read up	on places / on any places	G	L
5	to think what	could have happened	G	G
6	student pitched in	to tidy	L	G
7	dawned on him	what had happened	L	G
8	have been	laid off	G	L
9	snows intermittently	in the town	G	L
10	as a rule	employees get a	L	G

1	has a tendency		to turn / to show		G	L
2	on a daily basis		which is		L	G
3	under an obligation / under any obligation		to help		L	G
4	laying down		the law		L	L
5	the rules		do not apply		L	G
6	no point (in) / no benefit in		digging your		L	L
7	have done yourself / have caused someone		an injury		G	L
8	a once in		a lifetime		L	L
9	pick your		brains on / brains about		L	L
10	not think		Mary is up to		G	L

1	look on		the bright	L	L
2	not believe		she had been so	G	G
3	is prone		to flooding	L	G
4	of the meeting / of this meeting		is twofold	L	L
5	how old / of how old		it is that / it is the / it is this	G	L
6	going to	the dentist annually / the dentist every year / the dentist each year		G	L
7	the advent		of the internet	L	L
8	not ashamed		to admit	L	G
9	who does		not have	G	G
10	be feeling unwell		if he had / had he	G	G

Notes

Notes

Notes

Notes

Made in United States
Troutdale, OR
04/01/2024

18864881R00058